CELEBRATING THE FAMILY NAME OF FREEMAN

Celebrating the Family Name of Freeman

Walter the Educator

SKB

Silent King Books
a WhichHead Entertainment Imprint

Disclaimer

This book is a literary work; the story is not about specific persons, locations, situations, and/or circumstances unless mentioned in a historical context. Any resemblance to real persons, locations, situations, and/or circumstances is coincidental. This book is for entertainment and informational purposes only. The author and publisher offer this information without warranties expressed or implied. No matter the grounds, neither the author nor the publisher will be accountable for any losses, injuries, or other damages caused by the reader's use of this book. The use of this book acknowledges an understanding and acceptance of this disclaimer.

Celebrating the Family Name of Freeman is a memory book that belongs to the Celebrating Family Name Book Series by Walter the Educator. Collect them all and more books at WaltertheEducator.com

USE THE EXTRA SPACE TO DOCUMENT YOUR FAMILY MEMORIES THROUGHOUT THE YEARS

FREEMAN

Freeman, the name rings wild and bold,

Celebrating the Family Name of

Freeman

A story of courage, a heart of gold.

It echoes through valleys, through rivers and plains,

Where the wind sings songs and the earth remains.

Born of the earth, yet kissed by the stars,

Freeman journeys near and far,

A name not bound by weight or chain,

A soul untethered, free from pain.

In the dawn of time, when worlds were young,

Freeman's spirit was already sung.

By the trees that whisper in morning light,

By the hawk that soars in endless flight.

For Freeman means more than a name alone,

It's a mountain climbed, it's seeds well-sown.

It's the break of dawn after a storm,

It's the warmth of fire that keeps us warm.

Celebrating the Family Name of

Freeman

Through trials, through shadows, and through strife,

Freeman knows the dance of life.

With every step, they leave their mark,

A spark of hope in the deepest dark.

The name recalls a road untrod,

A call to wander, a gaze toward God.

To be Freeman is to break the mold,

To seek the truth, both young and old.

When shackles fall and chains are gone,

Freeman walks, forever strong.

Through meadows green or deserts bare,

Their heart is open, their soul laid bare.

But Freeman, too, is soft and kind,

With eyes that see, with heart and mind.

They listen well, they love with grace,

Celebrating the Family Name of

Freeman

With open arms, they embrace.

The wind that howls, the rain that falls,

Freeman answers nature's calls.

A spirit wild yet calm and free,

Like the eagle flying over the sea.

In family bonds, their roots are found,

Firm in the soil, deep in the ground.

But even as they stand their ground,

.

Freeman's soul still knows no bound.

ABOUT THE CREATOR

Walter the Educator is one of the pseudonyms for Walter Anderson. Formally educated in Chemistry, Business, and Education, he is an educator, an author, a diverse entrepreneur, and he is the son of a disabled war veteran. "Walter the Educator" shares his time between educating and creating. He holds interests and owns several creative projects that entertain, enlighten, enhance, and educate, hoping to inspire and motivate you. Follow, find new works, and stay up to date with Walter the Educator™

at WaltertheEducator.com

Milton Keynes UK
Ingram Content Group UK Ltd.
UKHW020127051024
449263UK00018B/570

9 798330 446445